By Jessiey James

Illustrations by Carolyn Mottern

POUNDS OF BABIES

To order additional copies of this book, contact:
Xlibris
844-714-8691
www.Xlibris.com
Orders@Xlibris.com

ISBN: Softcover 978-1-6698-0910-4
Hardcover 978-1-6698-0911-1
EBook 978-1-6698-0909-8

Print information available on the last page

Rev. date: 02/08/2022

Dedication: To Gabriella, Brandon and Jarrett

MOVING CO.

My brother, Jared, and I are bouncing around in the backyard. We notice a large yellow truck pull out of the neighbor's driveway. Gabby is no longer our neighbor. Gabby's family broke up. Our mom, Jessie, says: "Gabby and her mom, Teagan, had to move to another state." We will miss playing with her.

The next day, another truck pulls in the neighbor's driveway. This truck is blue. Out jump two small girl puppies. They look like us. Immediately they run over and say hi.

While their dad, Wiley, is pulling stuff out of the blue truck, we all stay in the backyard and play. One girl, Dillon likes to do cartwheels. Her sister, Delaney, can do a back walkover. We jump on a mini-trampoline.

A red car pulls in the neighbor's driveway. Dillon and Delaney run over to the car. It is their mom, Kelley. An extremely huge family pet jumps out of the backseat. It starts barking. It licks Dillon's arm.

Jared and I run over and ask: "Are we allowed to see your pet?" Kelley remarks: "Yes. I had better hold her down. She's snappy and going to have babies!" Jared says: "Babies!! How many?" She remarks: "We don't know. Maybe she will have one. Or maybe she will have 12."

Later in the evening, we notice Wiley put the pet in the backyard. Their backyard has a gold chain fence. Wiley says: "I'm going to be setting up a large kennel for the pet inside the backyard, but not today. I'm wiped out from moving furniture and boxes."

Jared and I are happy we got new neighbors. They have two girl puppies to play with. Even better, is their pet is going to have babies! What we do not like is their dog's name. Jared remarks: "Their dog's name is Puke?" We both laugh.

Jared asks our dad, Robbie: "What's a kennel?" Our dad remarks: "It's sort of like a playpen. It's a place for a pet to run around in." He says: "Why?" Jared says: "The neighbors are going to put Puke in one." Our dad laughs. I say: "Their dog's name is Puke." Our dad says: "Oh, well that sounds better."

Dillon says: "Puca may have jumped the fence in the middle of the night." They are very worried. Wiley says: "I hope she didn't go have her babies. We may not be able to find them."

Luckily, we spot the pet, in the alley behind the house. Our dad and us run back to the neighbor's house and tell them Puke is in the back. Our dad says: "While it looks like she managed to jump over the fence to get out of the yard, she will not jump over it to get back in. She's waiting at the fence."

Their family is glad to get their pet back. They decide to give her a bath in the backyard. The whole yard is full of white soapsuds. They are everywhere even on the tree branches. Jared notices a bubble on the weathervane on top of the garage.

Delaney says: "I heard you call our pet Puke." Dillon says: "Our pet's name is Puca, not Puke!" Jared and I look at each other and smile. Dillon makes Jared and I each say the name Puca until we get it right. Delaney says: "Now that sounds better."

Delaney and Dillon call Jared and I on the phone. They invite us over. We get to see their baby pets that were just born last night. Wiley says we cannot get too close yet. There are seven that are the same colors as in a rainbow. The tiny babies are red, orange, yellow, green, blue, indigo and violet. There are five that are pure white. In addition, there are four that are brown.

Seven plus five equals 12. Moreover, 12 plus four equals 16. That is many babies. Jared remarks: "I remember 16 ounces equals a pound. So, we have ourselves a pound of babies here!" I tell him: "Each baby might weigh a pound so we could have 16 pounds."

The next day when Jared and I go out to the backyard, we notice there are no babies in the kennel. It is empty except for Puca. Jared and I run in the house crying. We say to our mom: "The babies are gone!" She tries to calm us down. Jared says: "We need to call the police."

After lunch, Wiley and the girls pull in the driveway.
They begin unloading their car. They have the babies. Jared
and I are so excited. All the babies are wrapped in blankets.

I ask: "Are the babies alright?" Wiley says: "They are good. They had to go to the Vet. If you two would like to help carry them back to the kennel that would be all right." Wiley lets us carry one at a time back to the kennel. Then we have to leave them with Puca, the mother of the babies.

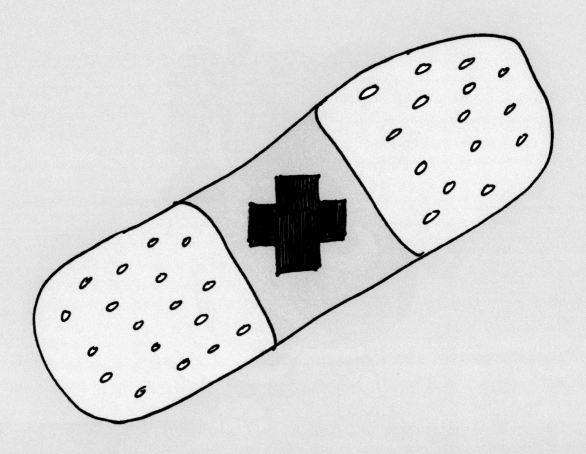

When Jared and I go back to our house, he says: "When I put down the baby I was carrying, its blanket fell off. I saw a big band aid on its back." I remark: "I wonder what that is for?"

At dinner, our mom explains: "The reason why the babies were gone and came back with band aids on their backs is because they had their tails cut off at the vet's office." Both of us gasp and say: "Ouch! I ask: "Why did they do that?"

Our mom further explains: "They are pedigree pets and that is what they do. Their tails will not be anything but a tiny stub. " I say: "Definitely not like ours as I twirl my tail up onto the table." My mom then corrects me. She says: "Don't put your tail on the table when we are eating."

Finally, when the babies are a few weeks old, Dillon's dad announces that we can all go in the kennel and play with the babies. We can hold only one.

Our mom remarks this is the funniest scene she has ever seen. She can't figure out who is running around inside the kennel more. Is it the babies or us? There are us puppies running one way and babies running another. Every time one of us tries to pick up a baby, they get away from us. They are great sliders and fast runners.

Oops, Jared drops the blue baby he is holding on its head. Our mother gasps and says: "On no, I hope it's not hurt. After all, they are supposed to be selling these baby pets for $450.00 each."

I wonder: "Will Dillon and Delaney have to take the blue baby to the hospital?" Our mom assures us the neighbor said the baby is all right. Now there are 16 babies in the kennel and all are asleep.

Printed in the United States
by Baker & Taylor Publisher Services